Sheila

I'm the mood for Norfolk [...]

Love & best wishes on your
Birthday Aug on

xx

Neville & Carol

NORFOLK
MOODS

NORFOLK MOODS

Terence J Burchell

HALSGROVE

First published in Great Britain in 2004

Title page photograph: *Great Bircham Windmill, located inland between King's Lynn and Wells.*

British Library Cataloguing-in-Publication Data
A CIP record for this title is available from the British Library

ISBN 1 84114 370 7

HALSGROVE
Halsgrove House
Lower Moor Way
Tiverton, Devon EX16 6SS
Tel: 01884 243242
Fax: 01884 243325
email: sales@halsgrove.com
website: www.halsgrove.com

Printed and bound by Oriental Press

INTRODUCTION

I was born in Kent and it wasn't until I got married that I moved to Norfolk. That was some forty years ago. When I announced to my parents that we were to move to Fakenham, in the heart of the county, they probably thought that we were moving to the flattest place in England, but that is far from the truth, especially around that lovely old market town of Fakenham and the north of Norfolk. Noel Coward's character of Amanda in his 1930 play *Private Lives* said 'Very flat, Norfolk', leading most people who haven't visited the area to believe that is the case. Certainly, there are flat areas especially in the west where Norfolk starts to take on the character of the Cambridgeshire Fenlands. The Broads to the east are situated in more rolling countryside, with some areas of flat land mainly on either side of the rivers and towards the coast.

Elsewhere, the county contains many areas of quite outstanding beauty, with some very steep, although not too high, hills. If you should wish to try cycling around the coast from Hunstanton via Blakeney, Sheringham, Cromer to Mundesley then I'm sure you will find the truth of that fact.

The history of Norfolk has given us many names of people who have shaped the world. From the Celtic Queen Boudicca (or Boadicea), George Vancouver to Lord Horatio Nelson (and Lady Hamilton), we find many who were either born or lived in Norfolk, and who became famous through their writings, explorations or being there when their country needed them most. The list is very long indeed, and in this book I have been able to only mention a few. Of those I have included I have shown the places they knew and loved and which may have influenced their lives, and ultimately ours.

If you have never been to Norfolk I hope that this book will whet your appetite for a visit, not just to the many attractive holiday seaside resorts that dot the coastline, but to those pretty villages, quiet country lanes and stretches of rivers and Broads that can be peaceful and relaxing, and where I know you will find a warm welcome. As I stated at the beginning of this introduction I come from Kent, the Garden of England. Think of Norfolk as being the playground!

Terence J Burchell

LOCATION MAP

Acknowledgements

I would like to mention those who have helped me with information for the locations of some of the photographs and to guide me with facts relating to the areas and connections with famous people.

Firstly, my wife, Vera, who has been most patient with me, especially when I have risen before dawn, stayed out all day, and arrived back after sunset, and then probably only bringing home one photograph. Mr Chris Alhusen of Bradenham Hall, for permission to photograph his lovely house. Mrs Bulwer-Long of Heydon Hall. The Norfolk Wherry Trust and *Albion*. Reflections of Norwich for the processing of all my films, and all those who have supported me during this project, I thank you all.

As a new day starts in Norfolk, the sun bursts through dark clouds which hang over the North Sea off the coast between Great Yarmouth and Gorleston.

The same sun but on a different day. This scene is taken from Acle Bridge looking into the rising sun which casts a romantic glow over the moored pleasure boats alongside the banks of the River Bure.

The City of Norwich is not missed by the touch of Spring. The Cathedral and the surrounding Close are tinged with colour, with the statue of Wellington rising proudly above the beds of flowers.

In the Spring snowdrops stand proudly by an old rotting tree.
The sun warms the ground and the flowers push themselves up to the light.

Soon the ground is covered with these pretty white flowers, now replacing the long-melted snow.

Bluebells add their lovely soft shades under the still barren boughs of the trees in this wood at Blickling Park.

Fungi, looking almost like sea-shells stranded amongst the bluebells.

*Soon more flowers join in as Spring moves towards Summer. Lynford Arboretum, between
Thetford and Swaffham, becomes a mass of daffodils spreading below the trees.*

*Here at the edge of a pond in the village of Mulbarton sits a
Canada Goose ignoring the yellow daffodils growing next to him.*

This pathway winding its way through Blickling Park invites a stroll along its length. Adjoining Blickling Hall the Park is a beautiful area to be in at any time of the year.

Foxley Wood, an ancient woodland, which is carefully maintained and gives great pleasure to those who walk there. Wildlife of many varieties live here amongst the trees.

*Fields at Barsham are bare at this time of the year, and are waiting for the seed the farmer
has sown here to push up through the soil and cover the fields with green shoots.*

This young Thrush sits on an old grinding stone contemplating,
perhaps, the long, hot Summer days now fast approaching.

Ashwellthorpe, a village close to Wymondham, contains some pretty cottages. This example proudly displays its Olde English country garden.

Top: *Walking along the numerous signposted paths is a popular pastime in Norfolk. Here, near Kirby Bedon, this group will eventually arrive at the edge of the River Yare at Bramerton.*

Lower: *The walkers may well be lucky enough to see the old Wherry* Albion *as she sails gracefully past.*

The Albion *passes by a young angler sitting on the bank of the Yare.*

There are other Wherries, but these were purpose-built as pleasure craft during the early part of the twentieth century.
The Olive and Norada are seen here passing each other on the River Yare at Whittlingham, just outside Norwich.

Olive, *with her identification letter 'O' at her mast head,*
and Norada *on the river at Thorpe.*

Norada *sailing near to the heart of Norwich on the Wensum,*
and passing part of the old City Wall, the Cow Tower.

Above: *Pull's Ferry, named after one of the ferrymen who once took people across the river here.*
Beyond its gateway stands Norwich Cathedral and the Norwich School.

Opposite: *Almost in the centre of Norwich the River Wensum passes modern developments,*
but the scene is still attractive with an old day launch having just passed under Fye Bridge.
From this bridge witches were 'tested' by ducking them into the water on a 'cucking' stool.

Above: *The rivers that flow around Norwich make their way eventually to the Broads, a series of man-made lakes left after digging out peat over many centuries. Today, however, Broads are still being made, now purely for people to enjoy either sailing, wind-surfing or just lazing on the beaches, as here at Whittlingham, just ten minutes' drive from Nowich.*

Opposite: *Walking or just sitting by the side of the Yare and watching the boats go by is a relaxing experience enjoyed by young and old.*

Most of the Broads have public access both on them or around the edges. Salhouse Broad attracts both people and wildlife. The Cordon Rouge pleasure boat is one way of seeing the Broads and rivers.

Swan, geese and pleasure craft stand side by side at Salhouse Broad.

Filby Broad, where it is said Scandinavian raiders settled and built their dwellings in the middle of the Broad.

Buxton, near to the old water-mill, offers a quiet stretch of the Bure where anglers can fish at leisure.

This Broad at Filby attracts all the usual water activities, but rarely gets crowded.

Between the River Yare and the Waveney a man-made waterway now known at the New Cut was driven. Here from Haddiscoe Bridge near to the border between Norfolk and Suffolk is a flat scene that most people associate with the county. Here, too, can be seen a typical Norfolk sky beloved by the Norwich School of Painters.

Top: *Another New Cut, this time near King's Lynn in the west of Norfolk and close to the villages collectively known as the Wiggenhalls, stretches out towards the area known as Saddle Bow.*

Lower: *Near to Wiggenhall St Mary Magdalen the Great Ouse fights its way against the strong winds that blow without resistance over the surrounding flat countryside.*

Above: *The village of Wiggenhall St Mary Magdalen and the church that gives the village its name, sits next to the Great Ouse.*

Opposite: *Approaching North Walsham on the busy B1150 one finds on the right side of the road a lovely stretch of water known as Captain's Pond, a natural lake that sits in a valley surrounded by trees.*

What waterfalls there are in the county are not spectacular. Although this one is certainly small it is set under trees on the River Wensum near Swanton Morley and makes for a pretty picture.

Lyndford Hall is found between Thetford and Swaffham. Standing above its lake, the Hall also looks out on a handsome arboretum. Here a great variety of trees, all identified by name plates, grow tall in an area of land open to the public.

Above: *The old Summer house that stands by the lake at Lyndford
is guarded by a loan goose standing proudly to attention.*

Opposite: *Blickling Hall is another that has a most attractive lake in the grounds on the edge of Blickling Park.
The old gnarled tree with the lone swan makes for a tranquil scene.*

*Here, in the middle of Mulbarton Common, this pond has a natural beauty of its own
as the sunlight strikes through the trees, the figures silhouetted at its edge.*

This horse and rider create a splash in the still waters of the ford at Glandford on the River Glaven.

*Nearby, another horse calmly contemplates the scene, while ducks
enjoy the Glaven as it gently flows towards Cley-next-the-Sea.*

Top: *At Pentney Lakes the pattern of trees and reeds are reflected in the still waters.*

Lower: *Marshland at Pentney, is home to many beautiful plants. Reeds, grasses and wetland-loving plants grow in abundance in these undisturbed areas.*

There are swans aplenty in the county. Here, at Thorpe, near Norwich, they eagerly await food while the pleasure Wherries, Olive *and* Norada, *their white sails echoing the swans' plumage, sail by.*

From the top of St Helen's Church in the village of Ranworth you can get views of the Broads — if you can climb the 89 steps, two ladders and a trapdoor that lead to the viewing platform. It is certainly worth the effort for this view of Ranworth Broad and beyond.

Malthouse Broad, again from the top of St Helen's, runs off to the right of Ranworth Broad.
On a clear day you can see, well, if not for ever, at least many miles.

St Benet's Abbey stands on the banks of the River Bure between Horning and Thurne. The Bishop of Norwich performs an annual ceremony of worship here, arriving at the Abbey by boat.

Above: *Dilham and North Walsham Canal was started in 1824 but was never a success. There were six locks in the nine-mile stretch. The canal was finally closed but the old locks can still be traced. This one stands at Briggate. There is a walk along parts of the canal, and Weavers' Way runs close by.*

Opposite: *In the west of the county stands Denver Sluice. It rises tall over the River Ouse keeping in check the waters that drain off the Fens.*

*On the River Wissey at Whittington canal boats, now used as houseboats, are moored against
the bank where the weeping willows bend down towards the water.*

On a hot Summer day horses stand quietly in a field next to the Wensum as it approaches Fakenham.

Running across a ford on the River Glaven this flock of sheep seem to have decided that the grass really is greener on the other side.

Here at Brancaster Staithe you can find fishing boats and private sailing yachts settling into the mud where the tide has receded, leaving just a trickle of water running away along winding channels.

At Wells the tide recedes a very long way. When the waters return the sea can pour back into the harbour at a great rate, and to a good depth, allowing the larger vessels to reach the harbour wall.

Approaching Wells-next-the-Sea one comes across the town sign which leaves no doubt as the sand, sea and tree-lined coast that makes this a most attractive harbour town.

Top: *The* Albatros, *a Dutch Klipper, lies alongside Wells harbour wall.*
This venerable vessel was built in 1899 and still sails today.

Lower: *Holidaymakers, such as this couple, attract seagulls whilst sitting eating*
their lunch and watching the comings and goings in the harbour.

*Catching crabs from the waters of the harbour
is a popular and pleasurable pastime
for children and adults alike!*

Blakeney, another very popular Summer destination for those who prefer rather quieter holidays. Here sailing, painting or just walking and enjoying the views is the order of the day.

It is from Blakeney or nearby Moreston Quay that you can take one of several boats that chug their way out to Blakeney Point to give visitors the chance to watch the Grey Seals as they either laze on the sand or swim around watching the passing boats.

Above: *The countryside around Sheringham and Cromer, both along the coast and inland, is far from the flat terrain of the Broads or West Norfolk. This hill is known as the Beeston 'Bump', lying at Beeston Regis.*

Opposite: *Sheringham is a larger town. The area is well known for its crabs and other shellfish and these can be bought freshly caught from the North Sea. Here, two local fishermen discuss their catch, or maybe just pass the time of day.*

From the top of the 'Bump' can be clearly seen, in one direction Sheringham…

…and, in the other direction, West Runton with its 'town' of caravans. Beyond in the far distance is Cromer.

The front at Cromer boasts a handsome pier with, at its far end, a theatre which hosts many shows throughout the year, and at which many well-known names from the entertainment world have appeared.

However, Cromer still retains its local industry of crab fishing. The reputation of Cromer crabs is spread far and wide and, as with Sheringham crabs, are considered the best in England.

Henry Blogg, triple VC of the RNLI, who died in 1957, was the coxswain of Cromer Lifeboat from 1908 until 1947. He also held the George Cross and the British Empire Medal. Many souls owed their lives to this man and his gallant crews.

As with many popular resorts Cromer can be quite crowded. Its beaches, though, are large and there is always plenty of room to enjoy a walk by the sea and breathe in the fresh air.

Further down the coast is enacted a common sight, that of yet another crab boat being launched into the waves. Seen from the top of the cliffs at Overstrand the figures with the tractor, that has taken the boat down to the water's edge, watch as the crew fight to take the craft further out to easier waters.

Not all fishermen have to go to sea to catch their own, or others', breakfasts. At Walcott a lone figure braves the strong, cold wind blowing from Scandinavia across the North Sea, but at least he has his feet on dry land.

The sea that can provide such a harvest also often takes something back. Along the coast at Happisburgh the waves of the North Sea, not always so gentle, have eaten away large slices of cliffs and the land beyond. In centuries past, whole towns have disappeared beneath the waves off the Norfolk and Suffolk coast. Houses at Happisburgh are going all too fast.

The Lighthouse at Happisburgh, with St Mary's Church echoing its shape pointing to the sky, is some distance inland from the crumbling cliffs. How long, though, before the sea is threatening both structures?

Above: *Returning up the coast to Cley we find that it is here that the river Glaven eventually finds its way out to the sea.*

Opposite: *Great Yarmouth, the largest of the Norfolk coastal resorts, has many and varied attractions, from its piers to the Pleasure Beach of noisy, colourful rides and sideshows. Even here, however, some people can find a peaceful place to sit.*

Cley's eighteenth-century windmill stands next to the Glaven. It may be recognised by many as one of the scenes from television with the balloon floating across the marshland.

Norfolk has a great number of wind-powered machines situated in a variety of buildings, many mistaken for windmills, when they could well be windpumps. On the River Thurne at Thurne Dyke stands one of the most attractive wind drainage pumps.

Above: *Yachts on the river give the appearance of actually sailing across the marshland as they approach Thurne Dyke.*

Opposite: *This delightful scene of anglers in front of the white-painted windpump standing out against a brilliant blue sky reminds one of long, hot summers spent beside such rivers surrounded by peaceful countryside.*

Above: *Clouds gather over Horsey Mill, which stands not far from Winterton-on-Sea.*
The evening sun warms the scene but the clouds warn of Autumn to come.

Beyond this misty blue field of flax stands Burnham Norton Windmill, not far from Lord Nelson's birthplace.

Another view of the windmill at Denver. An apple tree stands laden with ripening fruit, the red apples standing out against the green leaves and contrasting with the mill and the blue sky.

Back across now to Denver in the west. Here, another windmill in perfect condition stands reflected in the nearby lake. Here also can be bought flour ground between the millstones driven by the sails turning in the wind.

Returning inland and nearer to Norwich, Wicklewood windmill, with its adjoining millers' cottages, stands as a testament to the work of the Norfolk Windmill Trust who look after so many of these fine structures.

Above: *Close now to the border with Suffolk, and just a short distance from Scole and Diss, is Billingford Windmill, here standing with its face to the sun.*

Opposite: *Old Buckenham Windmill, not too many miles away, another example of the Trust's work of conservation. This is reputed to be the fattest windmill in the country!*

*Not all mills relied on the wind for operation. At Little Cressingham, near to Swaffham,
this mill has been operated by either wind, water or oil in its lifetime.*

Cringleford retains just one part of the watermill that once straddled the River Yare and was burnt down some years ago. The remaining building is now a private residence.

Newcomers to the 'Rotary Club' are the wind generators, now springing up across the county and the country, even off our coastline. This line stands on the horizon spinning away over a field of corn at Somerton. Are they generating the power that drives the machinery that grinds the corn to make the flour and heats the ovens that bake the bread...?

Every year throughout the area demonstrations take place of old machinery that once was a common sight on our farms. Here at Banham a crowd gathers to watch corn being threshed in the old fashioned way.

The threshing machine is being driven by a magnificent Burrell compound traction engine.
The belt whizzes and flaps around to the sound of this powerful, gleaming monster.

Standing patiently, this heavy horse, once a regular sight in the fields helping to carry great loads, pull the plough or other farm implements, again becomes part of a farming scene rarely observed today.

Sheep are raised in their thousands on farms around the county. At Intwood this flock, a mixture of black and white, graze contentedly.

Farms throughout Norfolk come in all shapes and sizes from the plain at Skeyton...

…to the fancy at Tacolnestone…

*…and the picture postcard as here at Bunwell. This was originally
a quite small arable farm that grew sugar beet and corn, but has
now ceased to support a farmer, the land being sold off to other
local farms and the house becoming a private residence.*

To give young people an idea as to how small farms used to look in the 1920s the Norfolk Rural Life Museum at Gressenhall runs Union Farm where the animals and implements of those days can be seen still working. There is also a farm cottage with the rooms fitted out as they were when the farmer and his family lived and worked there.

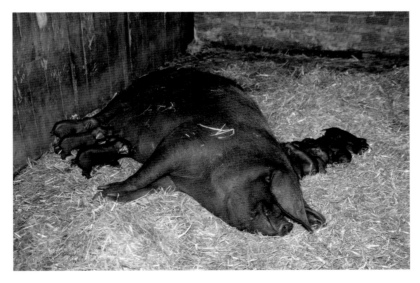

Top: *Two Suffolk Punches, Bowler and Trojan, are a popular sight with visitors, and can be seen working in the fields or pulling carts around the farm.*

Lower: *The livestock include Large Black pigs: the litter of this sow seem to be taking it in turn to feed or sleep.*

*Modern machinery has taken over from the small tractors of yesteryear and many very expensive machines
have air-conditioned cabs with satellite guided controls. Occasionally one can still see
an old Allis Chalmers tractor faithfully working on the land.*

Sugar beet is one of the most important crops in Norfolk. There are a number of sugar beet factories in the area, the largest being situated at Whissington producing many tons of sugar.

Corn-on-the-cob ripens in a field close to Norwich. There are a number of enterprising farmers who cut pathways into the masses of stalks and create a 'Maze of Maize', charging admission to the public.

Horses from a riding stable at Keswick near to Norwich graze peacefully in this tree-studded parkland.

Opposite: *Mulbarton has the largest village common in the county and is made much use of as an area for relaxing and recreation.*

Above: *In high Summer this cottage looks out across the Common with its masses of wild flowers and tall grasses.*

Opposite: *Cottage gardens can still be found that reminds one of scenes that might only be found in paintings. This garden at Intwood is certainly one.*

Here butterflies and bees are attracted to Dahlias…

...or to Sunflowers...

...and to the elegant Foxglove.

Decay, however, can also create beauty as here on a dying Beech tree which now supports a bracket fungus.

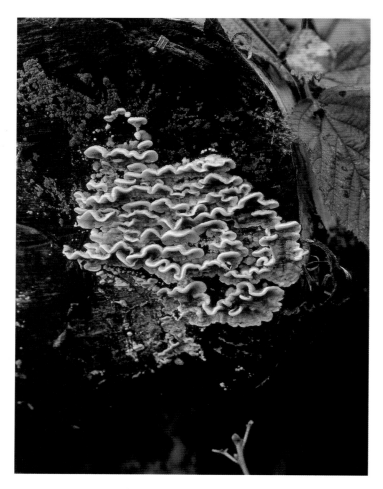

From another dead tree this mass of fungus looks like waves rippling on a pond.

A Ladybird puts a touch of scarlet on this fungus growing on rotting wood.

Shaggy inkcap, although lacking colour, still has a mystical beauty of its own.

The Fly Agaric, however, is a burst of colour as it stands under trees in Thetford Forest.

Colour is everywhere. Rape gives a carpet of yellow beneath a Norfolk sky at Hethel.

Yellow is also the colour of the wild Iris, or Flag, which is found standing with its roots in water at the edge of one of the Broads.

The Poppy is one of the most popular of flowers, whether in small bunches or, as here, in a great swathe in a field at East Carleton.

This combination of red Poppies and blue Flax give an almost three-dimensional quality to this photograph taken at the roadside at Keswick.

Bands of green, red, white and yellow appear to have come straight from an artist's palette.
It has happened here because consecutive crops over the years have self-set their seeds.

Here I have used a 'fish-eye' lens which produces an image covering a very wide angle, but at the same time creating excessive curvature to normally straight lines. Concentrating on the nearest poppies has given this photograph a perspective not normally seen in nature.

Not far up the coast, taken from a high point, this time at Salthouse Heath,
is this view of Salthouse and the church of St Nicholas.

Norfolk's history throws up many well-known names. This hill at Quidenham was believed to be the resting place of Queen Boadicea (or Boudicca). It does, in fact, contain an old ice house that was once used by the residents of Quidenham Hall, now a Carmelite Retreat.

*King's Lynn, where George Vancouver was born
in 1757. When George was just thirteen years old
he sailed with Captain Cook on the* Resolution.
*Vancouver gave his name to Vancouver Island,
the City of Vancouver in British Columbia, and
Fort Vancouver in Washington State.*

*East Dereham, now known just as Dereham, has its links with William Cowper, poet, George Borrow, author, and Edmund Bonner,
Chaplain to Cardinal Wolsey. It was Bonner who persecuted the Protestants, sending many men to burn in the fires at Smithfield.
This old building was erected in 1502 and Edmund Bonner was said to have stayed there. It is now the local museum.*

Thomas Paine, author of such works as The Rights of Man, *which caused much controversy being a defence of the French Revolution and republican principles, was born here at Thetford, where his statue now proudly stands.*

I wondered as I photographed the ruins of Thetford Priory whether Thomas Paine ever wandered amongst its crumbling walls…

…and even sat in the shade of the remaining tall pillars to write down his beliefs.

Standing at the entrance to the historical village of Castle Acre, and still in fine condition, is the gateway to the old castle through which must have passed knights and men-at-arms.

*The Priory at Castle Acre was founded by William de Warrene. Standing in approximately 36 acres it is kept
in remarkably good condition and the visitor can easily trace the various parts of the original buildings.
The prior's house is an almost complete Tudor building with rooms, oak beams and oriel windows.*

This photograph emphasises the completeness of the layout of the old building's walls, with beyond the prior's house.

From a latticed upper storey window in the chamber of the prior's house can be seen further finely detailed portions of the Priory.

Throughout the county ruins of ancient fortified houses and castles can be seen. Great Yarmouth has traces of eleven towers that were part of its walled defence. The north-west tower stands alone beside the river Bure.

William de Warrenne also constructed Weeting Castle. The church that stands beyond the castle walls is St Mary's, the tower of which was rebuilt in 1868 replacing the original Norman one.

Baconsthorpe Castle, built by Sir John Heydon during the Wars of the Roses as a fortified hall, is partly surrounded by a moat.

Caister Castle, inland from Caister-on-Sea, built by Sir John Fastolfe who led the English archers at Agincourt.
The castle is now home to a collection of classic motorcars.

War has touched Norfolk in many ways. The USAAF had many airbases here. Our own forces were trained in parts of the county, and still are to this day. A memorial to the Desert Rats stands beside the road from Thetford to Swaffham in an area used for exercises before our troops were sent to the Normandy beaches. Other areas of Thetford have appeared in the television series of 'Dad's Army' which, in its own way, was a salute to those who had to stay at home, but were always at the ready.

The plaque gives the dates and name of the invasion of Normandy at Gold Beach. There isn't enough room to tell the many stories of bravery which this monument really stands for, nor for the names of the men who took part.

The most famous name that is connected with Norfolk and the sea is that of Admiral Horatio Nelson, KB.
Born 29 September, 1758 in the village of Burnham Thorpe, he was the fifth son of the
Rev. Edmund Nelson's eleven children. The local public house is named the 'Lord Nelson',
although it was originally called 'The Plough', being built a hundred years before Horatio was born.

This is the Rev. Nelson's church of All Saints, and it is here that many of his son's heroic deeds are recorded along with memorabilia from his famous battles. Although his father lies here, Horatio is many miles away in St Paul's Cathedral in London.

Outside another church of All Saints in Upper Sheringham stands a curious memorial. It is a fountain fed by water that arises from high ground above the village and it commemorates the Peace that came to Europe when Napoleon was exiled to Elba.

Churches, it seems, can sometimes come along in twos! Here are two in the same churchyard. They are St Mary's of Reepham and St Michael and All Angels of Whitwell, although only one is now used for services. There was a third, that of Hackford, but this was burnt down in 1543 and only a few stones remain.

Above: *Thatching is still practised in East Anglia, the intricate patterns that are produced by the thatching craftsman or woman give the roofs of these houses a most attractive appearance. Much of the materials used are grown locally.*

Opposite: *The gatehouse at the entrance to Intwood Hall is built with cobbled walls against which roses grow, making a pretty picture.*

*Here, at Burnham Overy, are some fine examples of the cobbled houses
found in the county, especially along the North Norfolk coast.*

At Langham (where a variety of objects, including paper weights and little ornamental animals, are made in a local glass-blowing workshop), more cobbled houses stand, their construction being both practical against the weather and attractive to the eye.

Larger houses such as Heydon Hall, which is situated in a lovely parkland estate, has at its gates the village of Heydon.
The village appears untouched by the centuries, with The Earles Arms public house and the church of Saints Peter and Paul
standing by the village green. The village has often been used by television companies for period dramas.
The Hall is connected to the author Edward George Earle Lytton, the name Bulwer-Lytton
being recognised throughout the world in the mid-1800s.

One of the most famous of
grand houses, Blickling Hall,
a fine Jacobean residence.
Here once stood the manor where
the Boleyns lived, owned by the
great-grandfather of Anne
Boleyn. The fine house we see
today was built by Sir Henry
Hobart, but Anne will always
be associated with the place.

Bradenham Hall near to Shipdham brings us back to Lord Nelson. Here it was that his sister lived and Horatio would often meet Lady Emma Hamilton here and walk in the grounds with her. It is said that, whilst here, his clothes would be washed and hung over a sweet-smelling bush that grew by the back door to dry and thus absorb the scent. Here, also, Sir Henry Rider Haggard, author of King Solomon's Mines *was born in 1856.*

This excellent example of a market cross stands in the centre of New Buckenham on the B1113.
One of the wooden posts still retains the irons used to hold ne'erdowells during their time of penitence.

*Another market cross, built in 1617, now housing the Tourist Information Office,
stands looking proudly over the Market Square in Wymondham.*

This mother and her foal were constructed by an artistic blacksmith outside his smithy at Heydon.

Anna Sewell, authoress of Black Beauty, *was born at Great Yarmouth into a Quaker family. Anna's birthplace
is now a small restaurant. She died in April 1878 just a short while after her book became a bestseller.*

Summer turns to Autumn. The leaves turn to a dazzling display of scarlet and gold, finally falling to cover the ground with colour.

*In Thetford Forest the golden leaves still on the trees are contrasted against
the evergreen pines that make up the main part of the forest.*

East Carleton. Winter's grip has fallen on the trees and the surrounding countryside. Although the lake has not quite frozen it seems that it will not be long before the ducks are walking on the ice that will cover the water.

Above: *As the winter sun dips towards the horizon it suddenly bursts through the clouds, silhouetting*
a derelict windpump that stands forlornly in the middle of marshland near Hickling.

Opposite: *In the fields and lanes surrounding Mulbarton village hoar frost etches the trees against a cold and clear blue sky.*
Spring may not be too far away but until then the walkers, braving the chill wind, wrap up warm.

*Now the sun struggles to pierce through the mist that covers Mulbarton Common, failing to warm the figure
that is shrouded by the cold, damp cloud, seen walking home over the snow-covered ground.*

*The City of Norwich glows in the light from the setting sun, throwing into relief the Castle, the City Hall,
the Cathedral with its spire rising above all, and to the right of the sun the Roman Catholic Church of St John.*

Sunset, finally, at Heacham. As at Yarmouth the sun is seen reflected in water. Here it is the Wash, where King John reputedly lost his jewels. It is at Heacham that John Rolfe married his bride Pocahontas in 1614. I wonder, did they stand looking out at such a magnificent end to a beautiful day?